An Exotic Black Seed Cookbook for Health Nuts

Rare Recipes for Nigella Sativa and Black Cumin Seeds

Developed Life Books
4884 W. Hardy Rd
Tucson, AZ 85704
US

An Exotic Black Seed Cookbook for Health Nuts

An Exotic Black Seed Cookbook for Health Nuts © 2016 C.K. Media Enterprises, L.L.C.. All rights reserved. No part of this book may be used or reproduced in any manner whatsoever, including electronic, digital and Internet usage, without written permission from the author, except for written quotations for critical reviews, or for excerpts used for similar works. The author of this book is not a mental health professional or doctor, and makes no claims to be. The author is not responsible for any consequences that may result from using this information. This book is for entertainment purposes only.

First Printing – 2016

An Exotic Black Seed Cookbook for Health Nuts

An Exotic Black Seed Cookbook for Health Nuts

Contents

An Exotic Black Seed Cookbook for Health Nuts 1

Introduction 8
- **Get My Books For Free!** 8
- **A Note About Measurements** 10
- **Other Useful Recipe Books** 10

Getting Started With Black Seed 12
- What it's Not 13
- Health Effects of Middle-Eastern Black Seed 13
- Cooking with Black Seed 15

Appetizers 16
- Spicy Chickpeas with Tomatoes and Spinach 16
- Chicken Vegetable Salad with Avocado Pesto 18
- Carrot and Fennel Salad 20
- Spicy Indian Red Peppers with Chickpeas and Tomatoes 21
- White Radish Salad 22
- Spicy Rice Pilaf 23
- Eggplants in a Spicy Sauce 24
- Crispy Fried Potatoes 26
- Quick and Easy Tomato Relish 27
- Flavorful Sautéed Green Beans 28
- Moroccan Chickpea Patties 29
- Baked Asparagus with Black Seeds 31
- Persian Chickpea Salad 32
- Simple Cabbage Salad 33
- Rice with Black Beans 35
- Sesame Spinach 36

An Exotic Black Seed Cookbook for Health Nuts

    Roasted Broccoli Salad 37

    Hummus With Spices 38

Main Courses 39

    Creamy Squash Soup with Black Seeds 39

    Bengali Style Cauliflower Potato with Black Seeds 41

    Fish in Spicy Tomato Sauce 43

    Indian Potato and Chickpea Curry 45

    Chickpea Chicken Stew 47

    Coconut Curry with Peas and Chicken 49

    Sweet Potato, Carrot, and Red Lentil Soup 51

    Persian Mushroom Stew 53

    Roasted Vegetables with Lamb 54

    Authentic Winter Stew with Chickpeas and Vegetables 55

    Chicken Stuffed with Rice 57

    Tasty Mystery Stew with Green Beans and Potato 59

    Chicken Pilaf with Vegetables 60

    Bean and Mushroom Stew 61

    Barley Soup with Vegetables 63

    Shepherd's Pie with Cumin and Black Seeds 65

    Vegetable-Beef Stir Fry 67

    Healthy and Flavorful Pumpkin Soup 69

    Baked Rice with Spinach and Coconut Milk 71

Baked Goods 72

    Nigella Flatbread 72

    Nigella Walnut Shortbread 74

    Nigella Seed Cookies 76

    Mini Mushroom, Kalonji and Feta Pies 77

An Exotic Black Seed Cookbook for Health Nuts

Indian Potato Stuffed Bread (Kulcha) 79

Traditional Naan with Black Seeds 81

Crispy Salted Biscuits, AKA Cookies, with Black Seeds 83

Sweet Potato Cookies, I Mean Biscuits 84

Gluten Free Cookies with Toasted Black seeds 86

Cheesy Cornbread 87

Black Seed Flavored Flatbreads 88

Black Seed Cupcakes 89

Cheddar Scones 91

A Message from Andrea 93

Introduction

Thank you a lot for buying this book! I hope it will assist with the incorporation of super-foods like black seed into your lifestyle. After you've done trying out these delicious recipes, please remember that a review on Amazon would really help me to keep going with all this.

Get My Books For Free!

If you bought this on Kindle for a couple of dollars (or on paperback for a few more) I greatly appreciate it. However, keep in mind you also have a chance to receive some of my products for free. This is by signing up to my mailing list. I will periodically run a free promotional tool, and I'll let my subscribers know whenever I do this.

In addition, everybody who signs up receives a FREE copy of my book: **The 20 Most Deceptive Health Foods**

The point of this book is to educate readers about what foods are actually healthy, and which ones are not.

It's a must-have to take with you to the grocery aisles.

You can join the exclusive mailing list right now at the following link:

http://www.developedlife.com/andreasilver.

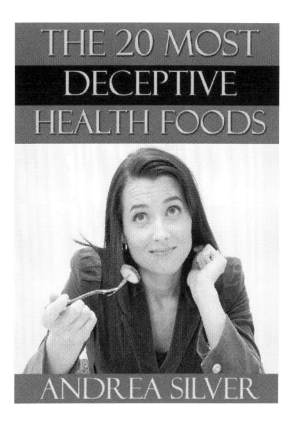

This is my completely free gift for my subscribers.

A Note About Measurements

I generally create these recipes using all or part of the metric system. This is more handy for exact measurements. There are many sites like metric-conversions.org where you can do conversions if you're not sure how to use metric or if you don't have a scale. If you are from the UK or USA and you are confused at all, go to this exact address: http://www.metric-conversions.org/volume/milliliters-to-us-cups.htm (this is for ml to US cups, as an example simply switch to UK cups or a different measurement that fits your country).

Through using ml this way for any type of recipe, you get exact amounts versus approximations.

Other Useful Recipe Books

I've created recipe collections for other "super foods" that are abnormally healthy and sure to be of long-lasting benefit. Check out:

My Turmeric Cookbook
(https://www.amazon.com/dp/B01AVY0EG4)

My Kale Cookbook
(https://www.amazon.com/dp/B01AVWG1WM)

My Salmon Cookbook
(https://www.amazon.com/dp/B01AI8RZCE)

My Hemp Cookbook
(https://www.amazon.com/dp/B01AX8486K)

An Exotic Black Seed Cookbook for Health Nuts

Getting Started With Black Seed

This book is going to work with TWO exotic Indian / Middle-Eastern spices that are often referred together as "black seed" due to their similarities. This is a confusing topic, as both these spices are different (with their own flavors), produced from very different sources, and yet are interchangeably referred. In researching this cookbook, I eventually decided that it was wisest to combine both kalonji (nigella sativa) with black cumin (bunium bulbocastanum, or Black Jeera); to create an essential list of recipes to make use of "black seed" in all its glory.

Therefore, as you begin cooking with these ingredients, take note of whether a recipe requires black cumin seeds or nigella sativa seeds. Nigella, which has a nutty, onion-like flavor, works amazingly well as a substitute for poppy or sesame seeds. It can be included in everything from salads, potato dishes, pastas, to baked goods. Nigella sativa creates a unique infusion of flavor.

Take note that nigella sativa often comes in different varieties. One popular form, that you can find at a lot of health food stores, is black seed oil. This oil can be used liberally in this cookbook, or as part of your every-day cooking habits.

Black cumin is not the same as nigella sativa. It has a smoky, semi-sweet flavor. It's therefore a bit less favorable for salads or baked goods, but perfect for larger entrees; such as various curried dishes, soups, sauces, etc. It's a popular ingredient across India, and yet is rarely seen in the West (much like nigella sativa, actually).

What it's Not

Nigella Sativa has no relation to marijuana named "sativa" and will, unfortunately, not get you high—you can try, but I doubt it will have too much of an effect (although it could, I suppose, if you smoked absurd amounts of it. Please don't.)

Further, nigella seeds have no relation to UK cooking goddess Nigella Lawson, whom indie chefs like yours-truly are stuck living in perpetual jealousy of. However, my recipes are still better tasting and healthier than hers are. If you don't believe me, take the "Andrea Silver-Nigella Lawson Challenge" and try two random recipes from either of our books and see for yourself!

Some other names for nigella sativa in particular include:

- Roman coriander
- Black sesame
- Black caraway

Health Effects of Middle-Eastern Black Seed

The Prophet Mohammed once said, "black seed can cure everything but death" (likely referring to nigella sativa). In recent months, black seed has exploded in the health food world as the latest wonder ingredient that can do almost anything, short of rubbing it on a stump to grow back a missing limb.

According to an index created by Green Med Info[1], black seed has been linked with healing properties to treat conditions such as:

---

[1] http://www.greenmedinfo.com/blog/black-seed-remedy-everything-death

- Chronic pain
- Bacterial infections
- Ulcers
- Asthma
- High blood pressure
- Inflammatory related diseases
- Fungal infections
- Hypertension
- Spasms
- Viral infections
- Diabetes
- Liver diseases
- Kidney diseases
- And cancers of various sorts

Among its health effects, black seed has been studied perhaps most potently for its ability to inhibit bacterial infections. This even includes the antibacterial resistant "superbugs" now plaguing hospitals across the world. Black seed also shows promise in fighting both fungi and viruses.

The healthy properties appear linked to three chemicals in black seed: thymoquinone, thymohydroquinone, and thymol. Together, these chemicals ward pathogens and / or help your body to eliminate pathogens. Combined with anti-inflammatory effects, it's easy to see how black seed is a disease destroying cocktail.

Studies into the benefits of black seed include a Croatian study that looked at the tumor fighting properties of two of these chemicals, with promising results[2]. A study into black seed oil's regenerative effects on the liver[3], studies into the antidiabetic properties of black seed[4], and many more studies of its anti-microbial effects.

---

[2] http://www.ncbi.nlm.nih.gov/pubmed/17080016
[3] http://www.ncbi.nlm.nih.gov/pubmed/23543440
[4] http://www.jofem.org/index.php/jofem/article/viewArticle/15/15

Based on this information, it does seem black seed could be the king of the superfoods, and a critical ingredient for anyone suffering from diseases that could benefit from a black seed rich diet.

Cooking with Black Seed

You'll find plenty of black seed supplements at the health store, but I prefer getting it the old fashioned way—cooking with it. Both black cumin and nigella sativa can be found in abundance through any online retailer like Amazon. The seeds can be added to almost anything that similar seeds like sesame would taste good on, and it's suggested to roast nigella sativa in a pan with a bit of oil before preparing it on your meal.

For this cookbook, there are plenty of Middle Eastern and Indian inspired recipes for you to enjoy. I included recipes that match closely with the origins of black seed as it has been used for thousands of years. This includes eggplant dishes, with chickpeas or hummus, curried dishes, soups and stews, pilafs, and of course plenty of baked goods where nigella sativa functions in a similar way as with poppy or sesame seeds.

Interestingly, this is perhaps the only black seed cookbook that I can think of. Despite how ancient the spice is, its popularity in the West remains negligible. It hasn't been until the last few months that it finally exploded on the scene—so I suppose we can expect to see a lot more of it soon.

I'm sure you're eager to begin. So let's dive into the recipes!

Appetizers

Spicy Chickpeas with Tomatoes and Spinach

The combination of flavors in this dish and its healthiness make it a great way to get started with black seed.

Servings: 4

INGREDIENTS

- 1 tbsp vegetable oil
- ½ tsp black seeds (nigella sativa)
- 1½ tsp fennel seeds
- 1 medium onion, chopped
- 400g can chopped tomatoes
- 3 green chilli, seeded and cut into qurters lengthways
- 2-3 tsp light brown sugar
- 1 tsp paprika
- 1 tsp turmeric
- ½ tsp black cumin
- 410g can chickpeas, drained and rinsed
- 1 tbsp tamarind

- 1 tbsp chopped fresh coriander
- 120 g baby spinach leaves

DIRECTIONS

- Add the oil to a large skillet and set over medium-low heat. Add the fennel and black seeds and fry for about 15 seconds.

- Add the chopped onion and sauté for 5-7minutes over medium heat until golden and translucent.

- Stir in the chillies, chickpeas, tomatoes, paprika, sugar, turmeric and black cumin, and bring to a boil.

- Then reduce the heat to low and let it simmer for 10 minutes.

- Add the tamarind, spinach leaves and coriander, give a stir and cook until the greens wilt.

Appetizers

Chicken Vegetable Salad with Avocado Pesto

A healthy, high-fiber salad with broccoli, beetroots, chicken breast, with garlic avocado pesto. Nigella sativa seeds add a good punch of flavor. The pesto itself is gourmet. The watercress also compliments the chicken. Make extra pesto for other dishes. **THIS RECIPE IS SERIOUSLY GOOD**.

Servings: 4

INGREDIENTS

- 250g broccoli, stemmed
- 2 tsp grape seed oil
- 3 skinless chicken breast
- 1 red onion, thinly sliced
- 100g bag watercress
- 2 raw beetroots (about 175g), peeled and julienned or grated
- 1 tsp black seeds

For the avocado pesto

- Small pack basil
- 1 avocado
- ½ garlic cloves, crushed
- 25g walnut halves, crumbled
- 1 tbsp rapeseed oil
- 1 lemon juice and rind

DIRECTIONS

- Cut the broccoli into florets and place in a pot of boiling water. Cook for 2-3 minute. Transfer to a colander and rinse under running cold water.

- Heat 1/2 tsp of the grape seed oil in a skillet. Add the broccoli and sear for 2 minutes per side until golden brown. Remove from the skillet and let it cool.

- In the same skillet brown the chicken on both sides, about 3 minutes per side. Transfer to a plate and let it cool. Then shred into chunks.

- Reserve 3-4 basil leaves for garnish and place the remaining in a blender along with walnuts, avocado, garlic, oil, 2-3 tbsp cold water and 1 tablespoon lemon juice. Season with salt and pepper and blend until smooth.

- In a bowl, sprinkle the onions with lemon juice and allow to sit for a few minutes.

- Place the watercress onto a large serving plate. Top with the onions and broccoli, followed by the beetroot and chicken chunks.

- Sprinkle with black seeds and lemon rind, garnish with basil leaves and serve with the prepared avocado pesto.

Appetizers

Carrot and Fennel Salad

Servings: 6

INGREDIENTS

- 2 large carrots, cut into thin sticks or grated
- 2 large fennel bulb, quartered and thinly sliced
- 1/3 cup cashew nuts, chopped
- Juice 1 lemon
- 2 tbsp olive oil
- 1 tsp mustard seed
- 1 tsp nigella seeds

DIRECTIONS

- Slice the fennel and place in a bowl along with grated carrots.
- Heat a skillet over low heat. Add the nuts and fry for 3-4 minutes until golden and fragrant. Remove from the skillet and allow to cool. Add to the vegetables.

- In the same pan, heat the oil and fry the mustard and black seeds about a minute. Add the lemon juice and mix well.

- Pour the mixture over the salad and toss to combine.

Spicy Indian Red Peppers with Chickpeas and Tomatoes

Packs a bit of a punch. Replace canned chickpeas with a fresh variety if you have them. You can also make tikka masala curry paste from scratch if you are ambitious. Black cumin / curry recipes can also substitute the normal curry.

Servings: 4

INGREDIENTS

- 400g can chopped tomatoes
- 1 tbsp canola oil
- 3 garlic cloves, thinly sliced
- 3 tbsp tikka masala curry paste
- 2 tsp nigella seeds
- 400g can chickpeas
- 460g jar roasted red peppers, drained, chopped

DIRECTIONS

- Add the canola oil to a large skillet and set over medium heat. Add the garlic, nigella seeds and tikka masala curry paste and cook for 40-60 minutes.

- Stir in the roasted red peppers, tomatoes, and chickpeas and bring to a simmer over low heat, about 10 minutes. You may add 2-3 tablespoons water, if the mixture is too thick.

Appetizers

White Radish Salad

Experience this simple and delicious salad with healthy vegetables, and spices.

Servings: 4

INGREDIENTS

- 1 large Indian white radish grated
- Salt and pepper
- 2 tbsp vinegar
- large pinch of sugar
- 2 tablespoons olive oil
- 1/2 tsp black seeds
- 1/2 tsp cumin seeds
- 1/2 tsp black mustard seeds

DIRECTIONS

- Grate the radish into a salad bowl. Add the sugar, vinegar, season with salt and pepper.

- Add the oil to a small skillet and set over medium heat. Add the cumin and black seeds and fry for 3-4 minutes. Once they begin to crackle, pour the oil and seeds over the salad and toss to coat.

- Enjoy.

Spicy Rice Pilaf

This dark colored pilaf is a combination of nigella sativa and black cumin. Further healthy ingredients like cilantro, cinnamon, etc makes this a nutrition POWERHOUSE recipe. Eat this every-day and live until age 120 (if you don't mind living long enough to see society taken over by androids).

Servings: 8

INGREDIENTS

- 2 tablespoons coconut or olive oil
- 1 large onion, finely chopped
- 2 cloves
- 3 cardamom pods, crushed
- 1 cinnamon stick, broken into 3
- 1/2 teaspoon black cumin seeds
- 1/2 teaspoon nigella seeds
- 3 tbsp fresh cilantro leaves, chopped
- 4 cups chicken broth
- 1/2 cup sliced almonds, toasted, for garnish
- 2 1/2 cups basmati rice

DIRECTIONS

- Pour the oil into a large saucepan and heat over medium heat.

- Add the onion, cardamom pods, cloves, cumin seeds, cinnamon stick and black seeds and sauté for about 7-10 minutes, stirring frequently.

- Stir in the rice, cook for a minute and then pour in the chicken broth and bring the mixture to a boil.

- Then reduce the heat to low and let it simmer for 20 minutes, covered. Remove the lid, cover the saucepan with a towel and put the lid back. Let the rice sit for 20 minutes.

- Fluff the rice with a fork before serving and serve sprinkled with almonds and chopped cilantro.

Eggplants in a Spicy Sauce

Eggplants are a staple throughout the Middle Eastern regions where nigella sativa and black cumin originate.

Servings: 4-6

INGREDIENTS

- 4 tbsp olive or canola oil
- 1/8 tsp ground asafetida
- 1/2 tsp skinned yellow split peas
- 1/2 tsp whole mustard seeds
- 1/2 tsp whole cumin or black cumin seeds
- 1/2 tsp whole nigella seeds
- 1/2 tsp whole fennel seeds
- 1 medium onion, chopped
- 2 cloves garlic, chopped
- 600-700 g Italian eggplants, cut
- 2 medium tomatoes, grated
- 1/4-1/2 teaspoon cayenne pepper
- 1 cup chicken stock or water
- 1 teaspoon salt

DIRECTIONS

- Add the olive oil to a saucepan and set over medium-high heat. Add the split peas and sauté until they become golden.

- Stir in the nigella seeds, fennel seeds, mustard, and cumin and cook for 30 seconds.

- Then add the onions and cook for 1-2 minutes. As soon as the onions begin to darken, add the eggplant and garlic.

- Cook for about 5 minutes. Stir in the tomatoes, cook for another minute and then pour in the stock or water. Season with salt and pepper and bring the mixture to a boil.

- Slow down the heat to low and let it simmer for 20 minutes, until the eggplants softened, stirring occasionally.

- Remove from the heat and enjoy.

Appetizers

Crispy Fried Potatoes

A few simple steps and these wonderful potatoes are ready to be served.

Servings: 6-8

INGREDIENTS

- 1/3 cup olive oil (divided)
- 1 teaspoon black seeds
- 1/2 teaspoon sea salt
- Flaky sea salt
- 1kg large sweet potatoes

DIRECTIONS

- Peel the potatoes and cut into cubes. Season with sea salt.

- Add 1/4 cup olive oil to a large non- stick skillet and set over medium-high heat. Add the potatoes, and gently stir with plastic spatula to coat.

- Put the lid on and fry over medium-low heat for 20-25 minutes, stirring frequently, until they acquire golden crust and softened inside.

- While frying the potatoes, toast the black seeds in a skillet over medium heat stirring occasionally, until fragrant and lightly golden.

- Place the fried potatoes in a serving dish, sprinkle with toasted tasted seeds and flaky sea salt, drizzle with the remaining oil and serve.

Quick and Easy Tomato Relish

This Indian topping can be served as garnish for a main dish, on rice, or even with chips or crispy pita. It's also a traditional recipe that uses nigella sativa.

Servings: 2

INGREDIENTS

- 1 small red onion
- 2 tomatoes, chopped
- 1 chili, finely chopped
- Fresh coriander leaves
- Juice from 1 lemon
- 1 tsp salt
- ½ tsp garam masala
- 1 tsp nigella seeds

DIRECTIONS

- Finely chop the tomatoes, onions and chilli and place into a a small bowl.

- Add the chopped coriander. Sprinkle with salt, nigella seeds and garam masala, drizzle with freshly squeezed lemon juice and stir well to combine.

- Serve with fried potatoes and pilaf.

Appetizers

Flavorful Sautéed Green Beans

This delicious side dish is full of protein and flavor. You can use any beans you prefer. And the best part is that it takes almost no time to prepare it.

Servings: 6

INGREDIENTS

- 900 g green beans, trimmed, cut
- 3/4 cup unsweetened coconut, shredded
- 1 1/2 tsp kosher salt
- 1 tsp black seeds
- 1/4 cup canola oil
- 1 tbsp yellow mustard seeds
- 24 curry leaves, torn

DIRECTIONS

- Add the oil to a large frying pan and place over medium-high heat.

- Once sizzling, add the mustard seeds and black seeds and sauté for about 1 minute, until fragrant. Add the curry leaves and sauté, for another minute.

- Stir in the green beans and cook for 5 minutes. Add the shredded coconut and 1 cup of water and bring to a simmer over medium–low heat 10-12 minutes, covered.

- Then remove the lid and cook the beans over moderate heat until all the liquid is gone. Season the dish with salt to taste and enjoy.

Moroccan Chickpea Patties

These spicy chickpea patties will melt in your mouth. Make sure you have all the ingredients at hand and get ready for this special treat.

Servings: 8

INGREDIENTS

- 1 small onion, diced
- 2-3 cloves garlic, peeled
- 1 tablespoon vegetable oil plus a bit for frying
- 1 can chickpeas rinsed and drained (or 1-1.5 cups cooked)
- 1 lemon, juiced
- 1/4 cup chickpea or oat flour + 2 tablespoons for coating
- 2 tablespoons parsley
- 1 teaspoon black seeds
- 1/4 teaspoon cinnamon
- 1 teaspoon salt
- 1/2 teaspoon ground coriander
- 1/4 teaspoon cayenne
- 1/4 teaspoon black pepper
- 1/4 teaspoon ground ginger

DIRECTIONS

- Heat the olive oil in a frying pan and set over medium-high heat.

- Add the garlic and onion and sauté until the onions are golden and translucent, about 4 minutes.

- Add the chickpeas to a microwave safe bowl and heat 2 minutes on High, until heated through.

Appetizers

- Puree the warm chickpeas, cooked onions, chickpea flour, garlic, parsley lemon juice, cinnamon, cumin, cayenne, coriander, ginger and black pepper in a blender.

- Shape the mixture into patties and coat them with flour.

- Add a few tablespoons of oil to a large nonstick skillet and set over a medium heat.

- Place the patties in the hot oil and fry for about 3 minutes per side until patties acquire golden crust.

- Enjoy

Baked Asparagus with Black Seeds

This makes for a healthy and delicious side dish and is quick to assemble.

Servings: 4-6

INGREDIENTS

- 450 g asparagus
- 1 1/2 tablespoons olive oil
- 1/4 teaspoon salt
- Pepper to taste
- 1 teaspoon black seeds

DIRECTIONS

- Preheat oven to 220 °C.

- Remove the woody root ends of the asparagus spears. Slightly peel off the bottom part of the spears and rinse in the cold water. Drain the asparagus and place on a baking sheet lined with foil.

- Season with salt and drizzle with olive oil. Roast in the oven for 10-12 minutes or to your desired doneness

- Meanwhile, in a skillet toast the black seeds over medium heat for a couple of minutes until fragrant.

- Remove the asparagus from the oven, sprinkle with black seeds and serve.

Persian Chickpea Salad

Servings: 4-6

INGREDIENTS

- 1 can chickpeas, drained
- 2 tbsp olive oil
- 1 tsp black seeds
- 1 garlic clove, chopped
- ½ tbsp grated ginger
- 1 lime, juiced
- 1 tomato, diced
- ½ cup cilantro, chopped
- ½ cup parsley, chopped
- Salt, pepper to taste

DIRECTIONS

- Combine the chickpeas, tomato, garlic, black seeds, ginger, chopped herbs, lime and olive oil in a salad bowl.

- Season with salt and pepper and toss well to combine and enjoy.

Simple Cabbage Salad

Cilantro and black seeds, as well as fresh thyme leaves and lemon juice make this simple salad healthy and flavorful.

Servings: 6

INGREDIENTS:

- 1 medium fennel bulb, stemmed
- 1 medium (900g) head of cabbage
- ⅓ cup olive oil
- 2 tbsp freshly squeezed lemon juice
- 3 tbsp red wine vinegar
- ¼ cup fresh thyme leaves
- 1 tsp salt
- ½ tsp freshly ground pepper
- 2 tsp mustard powder
- 2 tsp fennel seeds
- 2 tsp cilantro seeds

DIRECTIONS

- Remove the core from the cabbage. Thinly slice the cabbage and fennel bulb and place in a large salad bowl. Using your fingers, break up the cabbage to separate the thin strips, and set aside.

- Grind the black seeds and cilantro seeds in a mortar and pestle until finely ground. Transfer to a small bowl.

- Add the olive oil, mustard powder, freshly squeezed lemon juice and olive oil. Stir well to combine.

Appetizers

- Add the mixture to the sliced cabbage and fennel, add thyme leaves and mix well to combine. Let the salad stand for 5-10 minutes before serving.

Rice with Black Beans

This recipe seems simple, with a simple name, but it's quite dynamic. Cumin, black seed, cayenne and garlic creates a flavor you have to experience for yourself.

Servings: about 3

INGREDIENTS

- 3/4 cup white rice, uncooked
- 1 tsp olive oil
- 400 ml vegetable broth
- 1 onion, chopped
- 2 cloves garlic, minced
- 1 tsp ground cumin
- 1/2 ground black seed
- 1/4 tsp cayenne pepper
- 3 1/2 cups canned black beans, drained

DIRECTIONS

- Heat oil in a large saucepan over medium-high heat. Add the garlic and onion and fry for a couple of minutes, until tender. Then add in the rice and sauté for 2-3 minutes.

- Pour in the vegetable broth and bring to a boil. Reduce the heat to low, put the lid on and cook for 20 minutes.

- Add the black beans, season with cayenne pepper, black seed powder and cumin, give a stir and remove from heat. Let stand for 10 minutes before serving.

Appetizers

Sesame Spinach

This simple dish features spinach, garlic, soy sauce and black seeds, thus being very healthy and providing you lots of vitamins.

Servings: 4-6

INGREDIENTS

- 1 tbsp soy sauce
- 1 tsp toasted black seeds, crushed
- 1 tsp rice vinegar
- 1 tsp golden caster sugar
- 2 garlic cloves, grated
- 450g spinach, stem ends trimmed
- 2 tbsp canola oil

DIRECTIONS

- Place the spinach in a large saucepan of boiling water and cook for 3-4 minutes until the greens wilt.

- Transfer to a colander and rinse with ice water. Drain and squeeze with hands to remove as much water as possible. Place in a salad bowl.

- Than make the dressing by combining soy sauce, canola oil, vinegar, black seeds, garlic, sugar, and pepper in a small bowl. Mix well to dissolve sugar.

- Pour the dressing over the blanched spinach and toss to coat

- Refrigerate for at least 1 hour before serving.

Roasted Broccoli Salad

Servings: 4-6

INGREDIENTS

- 1 head broccoli, cut into florets
- 2 tsp lemon zest, divided
- 2 tbsp lemon juice
- 2 cloves garlic, minced
- 1 tsp black seeds, toasted
- 1/4 cup olive oil, or more to taste, divided
- Salt and ground black pepper to taste

DIRECTIONS

- Preheat oven to 230 °C.

- In a large bowl, combine the broccoli, 1 teaspoon lemon zest and 1 tablespoon olive oil. Season with salt and pepper to taste and mix well to coat.

- Transfer the broccoli to a large baking dish lined with parchment and roast in the oven for 18-20 minutes, until golden-brown. Let it cool and transfer to a salad bowl.

- Meanwhile toast the black seeds in a dry skillet until light golden and fragrant. Let them cool.

- Whisk lemon juice and garlic together in a small bowl, season with salt and pepper and pour over the roasted broccoli. Sprinkle with black seeds and mix well to combine.

Appetizers

Hummus With Spices

Hummus infused with spices, tomato, etc.

Servings: 4-6

INGREDIENTS

- 800 g fresh hummus
- 2 tbsp olive oil
- 1 tsp black seeds
- 1 garlic clove, chopped
- ½ tbsp. cayenne pepper
- 1 lime, juiced
- 1 tomato, diced
- ½ cup cilantro, chopped
- ½ cup parsley, chopped
- Salt, pepper to taste

DIRECTIONS

- Combine the hummus, tomato, garlic, black seeds, cayenne, herbs, lime and olive oil in a salad bowl.

- Serve with pita bread.

Main Courses

Creamy Squash Soup with Black Seeds

Nigella seeds are a flavorful addition to this winter soup; which brings a slightly strong flavor equivalent to using mustard seeds in similar recipes.

Servings: 4

INGREDIENTS

- 2 tbsp olive oil
- 1 onion
- 2 tsp nigella seeds
- A pinch of chili powder
- 800g squash, peeled, deseeded and cut into chunks
- 1 potato, cubed
- 850 ml vegetable broth
- Small bunch flat-leaf parsley

DIRECTIONS

- Add the olive oil to a large saucepan and set over medium heat. Then add the onion and sauté until golden.

- Stir in the black seeds and chili powder and cook for 30-60 seconds.

- Add the chopped potato, squash and vegetable broth and bring the soup to a boil.

- Then reduce the heat to low and let it simmer for 18-20 minutes until the vegetables are soft.

- Blend the soup in batches adding fresh parsley to a blender.

- Then return back to the saucepan and cook for 3-4 minutes.

- Ladle into serving bowls and enjoy.

Bengali Style Cauliflower Potato with Black Seeds

The Bengali region of India is known for their use of nigella seeds. This recipe combines them with other flavorful ingredients to create one of the most flavorful cauliflower dishes you'll ever have. (Of course, it's not hard to make cauliflower flavorful—simply add something that has flavor to it. It's kind of like the food equivalent of a chalkboard.)

Servings: 3-4

INGREDIENTS

- 1 large cauliflower, cut florets
- 2 medium potatoes, cubed
- 2 tablespoons olive oil, or you can even try mustard oil
- 1 teaspoon nigella seeds
- ½ teaspoon mustard seeds
- 3-4 green chili, thinly sliced
- 1/2 teaspoon sugar
- 1/2 bunch of the coriander, chopped
- 1 small tomato, thinly sliced
- Salt to taste

DIRECTIONS

- Add the oil to a cast iron pan and set over medium heat. Add the black seeds and fry for 1-2 minutes over medium heat until fragrant.

- Then add the green chili, mustard seeds, and nigella seeds.

- When the seeds become toasted a bit, throw in the cauliflower florets and cubed potatoes. Season with salt and sugar and stir with a wood spoon. Cook over medium-high heat for 10 minutes, until the veggies begin to darken at the edges.

- Add 1/4 cup water or as needed, reduce the heat to low and let it simmer, covered, until the veggies are tender and all the liquid has evaporated, about 15 minutes.

- Drizzle with little oil and stir to coat. Remove from the heat.

- Enjoy.

Fish in Spicy Tomato Sauce

A very tasty and aromatic dish loaded with Indian spices. A perfect dish to frighten your relatives (especially if you use a whole fish, head included).

Servings: 4

INGREDIENTS

- 400g-500g white fish fillets
- ½ tsp turmeric powder
- ½ tsp salt for marinade
- Juice of 1 lemon
- 1 tbsp dried fenugreek leaves
- ½ tsp nigella seeds
- ½ tsp cumin seeds
- 8 tomatoes
- 2-4 green chilies, finely sliced
- 1 tsp heaped red chilli flakes
- 5-6 cloves crushed garlic
- 1 tsp salt
- Handful of chopped cilantro

DIRECTIONS

- Slice the fish into large pieces and place in a bowl. Season with the salt, and turmeric powder, drizzle with the lemon juice, cover and set aside.

- Add about 3 tablespoons oil to a large saucepan and set over heat. When it begins to sizzle, add the nigella, cumin seeds and fenugreek and cook until they begin to darken.

- Add the garlic and cook for 30-50 seconds. Stir in the red chili flakes and salt, give a nice stir and add chopped tomatoes. Cook for 10 minutes over medium-high heat.

- Then place the fish fillets in the saucepan and gently stir with a spoon to coat.

- Reduce the heat to low and let it simmer until the fish flakes easily with a fork.

- Place in a serving plate, garnish with green chilies and cilantro and serve with naan or chapatti.

Indian Potato and Chickpea Curry

This is as good as it gets. Can be used as a currency if you are low on money (separate into kilogram bags and trade for goods and services), although some would argue one cannot put a monetary value to a dish this good.

Servings: 4

INGREDIENTS

- 1 can chickpeas
- 2 small potatoes, cut
- 1 onion diced
- 1 tsp cumin seeds
- 1/2 tsp nigella seeds
- 2-3 cloves
- 4 black peppers
- 2 cm ginger, grated, or 2 tsp ginger paste
- 4 cloves garlic, crushed
- 1 tbsp coriander powder
- 1 1/2 tbsp red chilli powder
- 1 1/2 salt or to taste
- 1/4 tsp turmeric powder
- 2 tomatoes finely diced
- 3 tbsp chopped cilantro
- 3-4 green chilies, thinly sliced

DIRECTIONS

- Add about 1/4 cup of oil to a large wok and place over medium heat. Add the black seeds, cumin seeds, cloves, peppers and fry for about 1-2 minutes, until fragrant.

- Stir in the onions, ginger and garlic, and fry for another 1-2 minutes, then add red chili powder, coriander powder, turmeric powder, and salt.

- Once the onions and garlic begin to brown, stir in the chopped tomatoes and continue cooking until the mixture thickens.

- Throw in the cubed potatoes and chickpeas, Give a nice stir and pour in 1 cup of hot water. Bring the stew to a boil, covered, over medium-high heat.

- Then reduce the heat to low and let it simmer until the potatoes are tender. Using a spoon, crush the potatoes and chickpeas to make a thicker gravy. Adjust seasoning to taste and remove from the heat.

- Ladle into a serving dish and serve garnished with chopped cilantro and green chilies.

Chickpea Chicken Stew

Enjoy this delicious stew full of heart healthy vitamins and nutrients. Great to serve with cooked basmati rice. If you are a vegetarian or are otherwise against chickens being eaten, substitute with tofu.

Servings: 4

INGREDIENT

- Olive oil or coconut oil
- 450 g ground chicken
- 1 tablespoon extra virgin olive oil
- 1 yellow onion, chopped
- 2 garlic cloves, chopped
- 1 green bell pepper, chopped
- 1 cup carrots, diced
- 1 cup celery, diced
- 1 (800 g) can diced tomatoes
- 2 (425 g) cans chick peas, drained
- 2 cups chicken broth
- 2 tsp black seed powder
- 2 tsp paprika
- 1 tsp coriander
- 2 bay leaves
- 1/2 teaspoon red pepper flakes, crushed
- Salt to taste
- 2 tbsp fresh parsley, chopped

DIRECTIONS

- Heat vegetable oil in a medium saucepan.

- Add the ground chicken and sauté for 10 minutes over medium heat. Transfer to a bowl.

- In the same saucepan, cook the onions and garlic until golden. Stir in the celery, carrots, tomatoes, black seed powder, paprika, coriander, bay leaves and red pepper flakes and cook for 5-8 minutes.

- Return the chicken to the saucepan, add chickpeas and chicken broth and bring the stew to a simmer over low heat, about 15-20 minutes.

- Before serving, remove the bay leaves and sprinkle with chopped fresh parsley.

- Enjoy.

Coconut Curry with Peas and Chicken

Everyone loves curry, and this method of preparation, with coconut milk and peas, won't leave anyone unhappy—except for sad clowns, who are paid to be unhappy.

Servings: 4

INGREDIENTS

- 1 tbsp brown sugar
- 2 tbsp canola oil (divided)
- 3/4 cup peas (frozen)
- 2 tsp curry powder (divided)
- 3 medium potatoes (cut)
- 1 cup carrots (sliced)
- 1 large yellow onion (chopped)
- ¾ tsp salt (divided)
- 1 tsp nigella seeds (black seed)
- 1 (400 g) can "light" coconut milk
- 1 (400 g) can reduced-sodium chicken broth
- 1 tbsp garlic (chopped)
- 700g boneless, skinless chicken breast (cut into cubes)
- 1/2 cup celery (chopped)
- 1/4 cup fresh cilantro (chopped)

DIRECTIONS

- Put the cut chicken fillets in a bowl, season with ¼ salt and 1 tsp black seed powder. Mix with hands to coat.

- Add 1 tbsp of oil to a large saucepan and set over medium-high heat. Place the seasoned chicken in the pan and roast, turning 1-2 times, until the chicken acquires golden crust on all sides, about 8-9 minutes. Remove from the pan and set aside.

- Adding the remaining 1 tablespoon oil to the saucepan, sauté the garlic and onion with nigella seeds until toasted, about 3 minutes.

- Add the remaining 1 tsp of curry powder and cook for 1 minute, until fragrant.

- Stir in the potatoes, celery coconut milk, carrots, broth, and the remaining 1/2 tsp salt and cook over high heat, stirring frequently. Once it begins to boil, reduce the heat to low and let it simmer stirring occasionally, until the carrots and potatoes have softened, 8-10 minutes.

- Place the chicken back in the pan and stir in the peas. Higher the heat and cook for additional 5 minutes, until the chicken is cooked through.

An Exotic Black Seed Cookbook for Health Nuts

Sweet Potato, Carrot, and Red Lentil Soup

This spicy red lentil soup is delicious anytime. The addition of carrots and cilantro adds a nice color and fresh look to this soup. Just don't spill any on your white shirt, lest someone think you've cut yourself.

Servings: 6-8

INGREDIENTS

- 2 tablespoons olive oil
- 1 large sweet yellow onion, chopped
- 1 large sweet potato, peeled and chunked
- 5 to 6 large carrots, peeled and chunked (about 4 cups)
- 1 cup red lentils
- 8 cups vegetable stock
- 1 tablespoon Harissa paste
- 2 teaspoons Ras el Hanout
- 1 teaspoon salt
- 1/2 teaspoon pepper
- Nigella seeds for garnish
- Cilantro, chopped, for garnish

DIRECTIONS

- Heat the olive oil in large griddle over moderate heat. Add the onions and sauté minutes until tender and translucent, about 7 minutes.

- Add the carrots, potatoes, lentils, harissa paste, ras el hanout, salt and pepper, pour in the vegetable stock and bring to a boil.

- Slow down the heat and let simmer, covered, until the lentils, potatoes and carrots are tender, 20-25 minutes. Remove from the heat and let cool.

- Blend the soup in batches until creamy and smooth. Adjust seasonings to taste.

- Pour the soup into serving bowls, sprinkle with chopped cilantro and black seeds and enjoy.

Persian Mushroom Stew

For those who flunked geography, Persian means regionally Iranian.

Servings: 4-6

INGREDIENTS

- 900g mushrooms, sliced
- 3 tablespoons vegetable oil
- 1 onion, chopped
- 2 garlic cloves, chopped
- ½ teaspoon powdered black seeds
- 1 tsp black cumin powder
- Salt, pepper to taste
- 2 tablespoons flour
- 1 cup almond milk

DIRECTIONS

- Heat the oil in a skillet. Add the onion and garlic and sauté for 2 minutes and then add the mushrooms.

- Reduce the heat to low and cook the mushrooms in their own juices for 10-15 minutes.

- Mix well the flour with the milk and pour it in the pan over the mushrooms.

- Cook until it begins to thicken then adjust the taste with salt, pepper and cumin powder.

- Remove from heat and serve it warm.

Main Courses

Roasted Vegetables with Lamb

Servings: 4

INGREDIENTS

- 1 tbsp olive oil
- 250g lean lamb fillet, thinly sliced
- 140g shallots, halved
- 2 large zucchinis cut into chunks
- ½ tsp black seed powder
- ½ tsp ground coriander
- 3 bell peppers (of different colors), cut
- 1 garlic clove, sliced
- 3/4 cup vegetable stock
- 1 cup cherry tomatoes
- Handful of cilantro leaves, chopped
- Salt and pepper

DIRECTIONS

- Add the oil to a large saucepan and set over high heat.

- Add the shallots and lamb and sauté for 3-4 minutes until golden.

- Add the zucchinis and cook for about 5 minutes until just tender. Stir in the black seed powder and coriander.

- Then add the garlic and peppers, reduce the heat to medium and cook for about 5 minutes until they become tender.

- Add the tomatoes and vegetable stock and let it simmer, covered, for 12-15 minutes, stirring frequently.

- Sprinkle the dish with roughly chopped cilantro and serve.

Authentic Winter Stew with Chickpeas and Vegetables

A nice combination of vegetables and spices. And it is also rich in proteins and vitamins. This stew is very filling and perfect for lunch or dinner. No side-effects will occur if it is consumed during summertime instead of wintertime.

Servings: 8

INGREDIENTS

- 2 teaspoons of olive oil
- 1 cup chopped onion
- 1 cup (1/2-inch) slices leek
- 1/2 ttsp ground coriander
- 1/2 tsp black seeds, crushed
- 1/8 tsp black cumin, ground
- 1/8 tsp red pepper, ground
- 1 garlic clove, minced
- 3 2/3 cups vegetable stock, divided
- 2 cups (1-inch) butternut squash, peeled, cubed
- 1 cup (1/2-inch) carrot sliced
- 3/4 cup (1-inch) Yukon gold potato, peeled, cubed
- 1 tbsp harissa
- 1 1/2 tsp tomato paste
- 3/4 tsp salt
- 450 g turnips, peeled, cut into 8 wedges
- 1 (430 g) can chickpeas, drained
- 1/4 cup fresh flat-leaf parsley, chopped
- 1 1/2 tsp honey
- 1 1/3 cups uncooked couscous
- 8 lemon wedges

DIRECTIONS

- Add the olive oil to a large pot and set over medium-high heat.

- Add the leeks and onion and cook for 5 minutes. Add black seeds, coriander, cumin, garlic and red pepper and stir-fry for a minute.

- Add the butternut squash, carrots, potato, tomato paste, harissa, turnips and salt, pour in 3 cups of vegetable stock and bring the mixture to a boil.

- Slow down the heat and let it simmer, covered, about 30 minutes.

- Stir in the honey and chopped parsley.

- Take 2/3 cup hot cooking liquid from the butternut squash mixture and transfer to a medium bowl. Pour in the remaining 2/3 cup stock, as well.

- Add the couscous, give a stir and let stand for 5 minutes, covered. Fluff the couscous with a fork.

- Serve the stew over the cooked couscous, sprinkled with fresh cilantro leaves.

- Serve with lemon wedges.

Chicken Stuffed with Rice

Mouthwatering chicken is paired well with rice, almonds, cherries and raisins. If you're a vegan, substitute the chicken with eggplant or pepper. But, I think that'd be a whole different recipe at that point. (Still good, though).

Servings8

INGREDIENTS

- 1 whole chicken
- 2 tsp salt
- 2 large onions, thinly sliced
- 3 garlic cloves
- 1 tablespoon olive oil
- 1/2 cup long-grain rice
- 1/4 teaspoon black seed powder
- 1/4 tsp cardamom
- 1/4 tsp cinnamon
- 1 cup chicken stock
- 1/2 cup sour cherries, soaked and drained
- 4 tbsp slivered almonds
- 3 tbsp raisins
- 2 tbsp fresh lime juice
- 1/4 cup apple juice

DIRECTIONS

- Wash the chicken and pat dry. Heat 1 tablespoon of oil in a skillet over medium heat. Add the onions and garlic and sauté for 3-5 minutes until golden brown.

- Stir in the uncooked rice, cinnamon, black seeds, cardamom, 1 teaspoon salt and pepper and continue cooking for another 5 minutes, stirring frequently.

- Next, pour in the chicken broth and cook over low heat for 12-15 minutes, covered.

- Stir in the sour cherries, raisins, almonds, and lime juice and remove the skillet from heat. Taste and adjust seasonings as needed.

- Fill the rice mixture into the chicken cavity, and tightly tie the chicken legs.

- Sprinkle with 1 teaspoon salt, a pinch of cinnamon, black seed powder, 1 teaspoon sugar and rub to coat evenly.

- Place the stuffed chicken in a baking dish, pour the apple juice over it all, cover with foil and roast in the oven for 45 minutes.

- Enjoy!

Tasty Mystery Stew with Green Beans and Potato

The mysterious ingredient is (spoiler)—nigella seeds.

Servings: 10

INGREDIENTS

- 450 g green beans, cut
- 1 tbsp olive oil
- 1 onion, chopped
- ½ tbsp nigella seeds
- 1 (800 g) can whole plum tomatoes, with juice or use fresh tomatoes
- 2 zucchinis, cut into half moons
- Garlic, cayenne, oregano and thyme, to taste
- 1 large potato, peeled and cut into cubes
- Salt and black pepper, to taste
- Freshly chopped parsley

DIRECTIONS

- Add the olive oil to a large saucepan and set over a medium heat. Add the onion and nigella seeds and cook for 3-4 minutes, until the onion is light golden and tender.

- Add the green beans, stir, and cook for about 5 minutes. Stir in the chopped zucchini, potato, tomatoes and garlic, and season with the garlic, cayenne, thyme, oregano, salt and pepper.

- Once the stew begins to boil, reduce the heat and simmer, covered, for about 20 minutes until the potatoes have softened.

- Ladle the stew into a serving bowl, sprinkle with fresh parsley and serve with toasted bread.

Main Courses

Chicken Pilaf with Vegetables

Although the word "pilaf" may sound like a less than flattering sound-effect, the recipes are quite good. If you're a vegetarian, try substituting chicken broth for vegetable broth, and chicken with tofu.

Servings: 2

INGREDIENTS

- 2 tsp coconut oil
- 2 small onions, chopped
- 1 teaspoon black seeds
- 1 cup basmati rice
- 1 cup chicken broth
- 2 cups fresh steamed mixed vegetables
- ½ cup frozen spinach
- 2 large boneless, skinless chicken thigh fillets, cut
- Salt and pepper to taste

DIRECTIONS

- Add the oil to a medium skillet and set over medium heat. Add the onion and cook for 5 minutes until tender.

- Stir in the cut chicken and brown for 3-4 minutes. Then add the rice and curry paste, give a stir and cook for a minute.

- Add the frozen vegetables and pour in the chicken broth. Once the mixture begins to boil, slow down the heat to low, put the lid on the skillet and cook about 10 minutes.

- Next, add the spinach, give a stir and let cook for another 10 minutes until the rice has softened and all the liquid is absorbed.

- Season the rice with salt and pepper to taste, stir and remove the pan from the heat.

Bean and Mushroom Stew

This makes a vitamin-rich and healthy dinner on cold winter nights. Contains a large amount of fiber which you wouldn't find anywhere else short of eating a wool carpet.

Servings: 4-6

INGREDIENTS

- 2 tbsp vegetable oil
- 900 g fresh mushrooms, sliced
- 2 cups canned black beans, drained
- 1 onion, sliced
- 4 garlic cloves, chopped
- 1 cup tomato puree
- 5 cups vegetable stock
- 1 tsp black seed powder
- 2 potatoes, peeled and cubed
- 1/4 tsp cayenne pepper
- 1/4 cup chopped cilantro
- Salt, pepper to taste

DIRECTIONS

- Add the vegetable oil in a saucepan and set over medium heat.

- Add the onion and garlic. Sauté for 2 minutes then add the mushrooms, black seed powder, cayenne pepper and potatoes. Cook for another 5 minutes.

- Drain the beans and add to the saucepan along with the tomato puree. Pour in the vegetable stock, and bring to a boil over high heat.

- Reduce the heat to low and let it simmer for 20-25 minutes until the vegetables become soft and the stew has slightly thickened.

- Stir in the chopped cilantro and serve.

Barley Soup with Vegetables

Barley has a high nutritional content and a nutty flavor that works great in soups, as well as stews or salads.

Servings: 4-6

INGREDIENTS:

- 2 tablespoons olive oil
- 1 onion, chopped
- 1 garlic clove, chopped
- 1 cup uncooked barley, rinsed
- 4 cups vegetable stock
- ½ tsp black seed powder
- ½ tsp regular or black cumin powder
- 1 lime, juiced
- 2 tomatoes, diced
- 1 carrot, diced
- Salt, pepper to taste
- 2 tablespoons chopped parsley
- 450 g chicken, cut

DIRECTIONS

- Heat the olive oil in a saucepan and set over medium heat. Add the chicken pieces and cook on both sides for 10 minutes. Remove from the pan.

- Add some more oil to the saucepan and cook the onion and garlic 2 minutes then add the barley, black seed powder and cumin.

- Sauté for 2 more minutes then stir in the tomatoes and carrot.

- Pour in the stock and season with salt and pepper and bring to a boil. Reduce the heat to low, return the chicken to the pan and let it simmer or 20 minutes, until the vegetables are tender and the chicken is cooked through..

- Stir in the chopped parsley, ladle into serving bowl and enjoy.

- Serve the soup warm and fresh.

Shepherd's Pie with Cumin and Black Seeds

This is a rich and spicy shepherd's pie with ground beef and cauliflower. Your family will love it, unless your family is terrified of weird ingredients like black cumin that you discover on bizarre cookbooks that you find late at night on Amazon.com.

Servings: 6

INGREDIENTS

- 2 tbsp butter 1/2 tsp pepper
- 1/2 tsp black cumin powder
- ½ teaspoon black seed powder
- 1 onion, finely chopped
- 2 tbsp lemon juice
- 1 kg ground beef
- 1 1/2 tbsp olive oil
- 3/4 cup cheddar cheese (grated)
- 1 tsp salt
- 2 small cauliflower

DIRECTIONS

- Preheat oven to 170 °C and gently coat a baking pan with oil.

- Cook the cauliflower in a pot of boiling water until soft, about 15 minutes.

- In a large frying pan, heat the olive oil and cook the beef until lightly golden. Then season with salt, black seed powder and pepper and let it cook, stirring occasionally, about 20-22 minutes.

- Finally add the onions and cook for additional 3-4 minutes. Drizzle the beef mixture with lemon juice, give a stir and transfer to the prepared baking pan. Spread in an even layer.

- In a bowl, mash the cauliflower with butter and spread over the beef. Sprinkle with grated cheese and bake in the oven for 15 to 20 minutes. Let stand for at least 5 minutes and serve.

Vegetable-Beef Stir Fry

This recipe requires you to carefully follow the order of preparation in the direction. Otherwise, the end result could be catastrophic. As usual, if you're a vegetarian or vegan, replace beef with tofu.

Servings: 2-4

INGREDIENTS

- 2 tbsp olive oil
- 1/2 tsp red pepper flakes
- 1/4 cup green onion, thinly sliced
- 1/4 cup soy sauce
- 225 g boneless beef sirloin
- 2 garlic cloves, minced
- 1 cup broccoli florets, sliced
- 1/2 tsp black seed powder
- 1/2 tsp ground cumin
- 2 tbsp cooking oil
- 1 tbsp sugar
- 1 cup cauliflower florets, sliced
- 1/3 cup cold water
- 1 tbsp cornstarch
- 1/2 tsp pepper
- 1 cup carrot, peeled, julienned

DIRECTIONS

- Thinly slice the beef and place in a medium bowl. Add the soy sauce, onions, red pepper flakes, garlic, olive oil and sugar, flavor with ground pepper and gently toss to combine.

- Let the beef marinate for about 30-40 minutes at room temperature.

- Then drain the meat and reserve the marinade for later use.

- In a small cup, dissolve the cornstarch in water, stir in the marinade and black seed powder.

- Add 1 tablespoon of cooking oil to a large frying pan and set over high heat. Add the carrots and fry for 3-4 minutes, stirring frequently.

- Add the cauliflower and broccoli and cook for another 2-3 minutes, until vegetables are just tender.

- Transfer the vegetables to another dish and cover to keep warm.

- Add the remaining oil to the same pan and set over medium heat. Then stir fry the beef in 2 batches until golden-brown on all sides.

- Then combine all the beef in the pan, add the cornstarch mixture and bring to a simmer until the sauce thickens, stirring frequently.

- Add the vegetables, cook for another minute and remove from the heat.

- Serve the dish with hot rice

Healthy and Flavorful Pumpkin Soup

This is a very tasty and healthy soup, full of spices and it is very simple to prepare. Your kids will love it. Just don't let them see the words "healthy" in the recipe title.

Servings: 4

INGREDIENTS

- 2 tsp extra virgin olive oil
- 900g pumpkin, peeled and seeded
- 2 leeks, trimmed and sliced
- 1 garlic clove, crushed
- 1 tsp regular or black cumin, ground
- 1 teaspoon black seeds, toasted
- 3 cups vegetable stock or water
- Salt, to taste
- Black pepper, to taste

DIRECTIONS

- Using a sharp knife peel the pumpkin and cut into coarse pieces. Add the oil to a large saucepan and place over medium heat.

- Add the leeks and garlic, and cook until tender.

- Stir in the cumin and cook for another minute. Add the pumpkin pieces, pour in the stock/water, sprinkle with salt and pepper, and cook over a moderate heat.

- Once it begins to boil, reduce the heat to low and simmer for 25-30 minutes, until the pumpkin has softened. Transfer the soup to a blender and pulse until pureed.

- Return the soup back to the saucepan and heat for 1-2 minutes. Divide the soup among serving bowls, sprinkle with black seeds and serve immediately.

Baked Rice with Spinach and Coconut Milk

I know I need to include more vegan recipes in this thing. Well, here's another one, at least.

Servings: 10

INGREDIENTS

- 3 tablespoons of a healthy oil of choice
- 1 teaspoon pepper
- 1 cup long rice
- 2 (13 1/2 oz.) cans coconut milk
- 2 teaspoon black seed powder
- 1 cup onion, chopped
- 1 1/2 tsp salt
- 2 (280 g) packages frozen spinach (thawed, chopped)
- 2 cups cooked brown lentils
- 2 garlic cloves minced

DIRECTIONS

- Preheat oven to 175 °C.

- Add the oil to an ovenproof pan and set over low heat. Add the garlic and onion and sauté until lightly golden.

- Add black seeds powder, rice, season with salt and pepper and cook for another 3 minutes.

- Stir in the spinach and cooked lentils and pour the coconut milk over the rice mixture. Put the lid on and transfer to the oven.

- Bake 35-40 minutes, until the top becomes light golden. Serve immediately.

Baked Goods

Nigella Flatbread

I must emphasize that these recipes have nothing to do with Nigella Lawson. I'm not calling her a "flatbread", although it may be apt to do so.

Makes 6 breads

INGREDIENTS

for the bread
- 2 tbsp olive oil (plus more for greasing)
- 15g / 1 tablespoon fresh yeast
- 1 tsp plain yoghurt
- 500 grams strong white bread flour
- 2 teaspoons salt
- 2 tbsp plain yoghurt
- 300 ml warm water
- for the glaze
- 1 large egg
- 1 teaspoon water

- 1 tbsp nigella seeds

DIRECTIONS

- Place the flour, yeast and salt in a large mixing bowl. Make a hole in the center. In a small bowl combine the yogurt and oil. Add the water and mix well.

- Pour the mixture into the flour mixture and mix well to form a soft dough.

- Transfer the dough to a dusted work surface and knead well with your hands. If the dough is still sticky you may add more flour, until it becomes elastic.

- Shape the dough into a big ball, coat with oil and place in a bowl. Cover with a clean kitchen towel and let it sit for an hour to rise.

- Once the dough has doubled in size, divide it into 6 pieces.

- Then using a rolling pin, roll out each of the balls into a thin flat oval. Arrange them on two baking sheets and let them sit for 15 minutes, covered with kitchen towel.

- Using your hands or a kitchen knife, make diagonal lines over the loaves then draw the same on other direction to get a criss-cross shape.

- In a small bowl, whisk the egg with yoghurt and water and brush the mixture over the top of the breads.

- Sprinkle with nigella seeds and bake in the preheated oven at 180 C until golden brown and firm to the touch.

- Remove from the oven and enjoy.

Nigella Walnut Shortbread

Does it regret being called "short"?

Makes 25

INGREDIENTS

- 250g butter, softened
- 1/2 teaspoon vanilla extract
- 1 ¼ cups plain flour
- 1/4 cup corn flour
- 1 teaspoons ground black seeds
- 1 teaspoons lemon juice
- ¾ salt
- 1/4 cup walnuts, finely chopped
- 1 egg, lightly beaten
- Sea salt flakes
- Freshly ground black pepper

DIRECTIONS

- Preheat oven to 180C. Line two baking sheets with baking paper.

- Place the butter, cornflour, flour, vanilla, walnuts lemon juice, black seeds, and salt in a large bowl and mix with an electric mixer to form dough.

- Dust your work surface with flour and place the dough on it. Knead with your hands and shape into two balls.

- Using a rolling pin, roll out the dough into a thin circle and cut with a round cookie cutter. Arrange on the baking sheets.

- Repeat the same with the second dough ball. Place the cookies in the fridge and let them sit for about ½ hour.

- Beat the egg in a small bowl and brush over the top of cookies.

- Then sprinkle the cookies with sea salt flakes and black pepper. Bake in the oven for 18-20 minutes until golden.

- Remove from the oven. Let them cool for 15 minutes and enjoy.

Nigella Seed Cookies

Makes about 36 cookies

INGREDIENTS

- 1.5 cup whole wheat flour
- 1/2 cup all purpose flour
- 1/4 cup semolina
- 1tsp. baking powder
- 1tsp. salt
- 1tsp. sugar
- 2 tsp. nigella seeds
- 1/2 stick butter, softened
- 1/4 cup milk

DIRECTIONS

- Preheat oven at 175 °C.

- Combine the whole wheat flour, all purpose flour, semolina, nigella seeds, baking powder, sugar, salt in a large bowl and mix well.

- Add the softened butter and mix with your hands until the mixture resembles coarse crumbs.

- Mix in the milk, a little at a time to form soft dough. Transfer to a floured surface and using a rolling pin roll out into a thin circle.

- Cut into rounds or other shapes with a cookie cutter and arrange them on a baking dish lined with parchment.

- Repeat this until all dough has gone. Bake in the oven for 25 minutes until risen and firm to the touch.

Mini Mushroom, Kalonji and Feta Pies

Servings 6

INGREDIENTS

For the filling:

- 500g Portobello mushrooms, sliced
- 100g feta cheese, crumbled
- 1 tbsp butter
- 3 cloves garlic, crushed
- ½ tsp black seeds
- 1 tsp lemon thyme
- ½ tsp black pepper

Crust

- 235g plain flour
- 55ml water
- 50ml skimmed milk
- 75g unsalted butter
- 1 tsp salt
- Milk and turmeric to brush the pastry lids

DIRECTIONS

- Melt the butter in a skillet over low heat. Add the garlic and black seeds and fry for about 1-2 minutes until golden and fragrant. Add the mushrooms and cook for 5 minutes, Stir in the thyme, sprinkle with black pepper and turn off the heat.

- Transfer to a colander to drain. Once cool enough to handle, squeeze out the mushrooms with hands to remove as much liquid as possible. Then mix in the feta and chill for 20 minutes.

- Preheat the oven to 160°C.

- To make the dough, combine the butter, milk and water in a medium saucepan and bring to a boil.
- Add the flour. Mix well and transfer to a work surface dusted with flour. Knead with your hands until smooth.
- Shape into 6 balls, then reserve 1/3 of each ball to use as a pie lid. Roll each of the balls into a circle and place in a cupcake tin, Press with fingers until the bottom and the sides are covered.

- Place about 1-2 tablespoons mushroom mixture into each of the muffin cups. Roll out the reserved dough balls and top the pies, pressing the edges with fingers to seal.

- Heat the milk in a pot, add turmeric, stir well and brush the mixture over the pies.
- Bake in the preheated oven for 35-40 minutes. Enjoy.

Indian Potato Stuffed Bread (Kulcha)

This a simple and tasty recipe for Kulcha or Indian stuffed bread. What better thing can one do with bread but stuff stuff into it? (I've always wanted to stay "stuff stuff").

Servings: 8

INGREDIENTS

For stuffing

- 2 pieces large cooked potatoes
- 1 onion, chopped
- 2-3 pieces green chili, chopped
- 1/4 tablespoon turmeric powder
- 1/4 tablespoon salt

For bread

- 1 cup all purpose flour
- Refined oil - for frying
- 1/4 tablespoon nigella seeds
- 1 tablespoon coriander leaves
- 2-3 tablespoon curd

DIRECTIONS

- Cook the potatoes for 20-25 minutes until tender. Drain and mash them.

- Cook onions and green chilli in 2 tablespoon of oil over medium heat for about 1-2minutes.

- Stir in the turmeric powder, mashed potatoes, and salt. Cook for about 3 minutes and remove from the heat. Let it cool.

Baked Goods

- To make dough, combine the flour, curd and 2 tablespoons of oil in a medium bowl. Add enough water to form a soft and elastic dough.

- Shape it into small balls. Sprinkle a work surface with flour. Roll out the balls into small circles, place the stuffing in the center, bring the edges together and seal. Flatten the bread with a rolling pin.

- Add oil to a tava and set over medium heat. Sprinkle the breads with nigella seeds and chopped coriander and cook them on both sides until golden on both sides.

- Enjoy.

Traditional Naan with Black Seeds

Use this recipe for any of the Indian recipes elsewhere in this book. Or be a rebel and eat it with non-Indian food.

Servings: 6

INGREDIENTS

- 175ml lukewarm water
- 1 teaspoon dried active baking yeast
- 1 teaspoon caster sugar
- 250g plain flour
- 1 teaspoon salt
- 4 tablespoons ghee
- 2 tablespoons plain curd
- 2 teaspoons black seeds

DIRECTIONS

- Dissolve the yeast in lukewarm water, adding 1 teaspoon sugar. Let it stand for 10 minutes.

- Combine the flour and salt in a large bowl. Pour in the yeast mixture, curd and 1/2 of the ghee. Mix well to form a dough.. Then transfer to a floured surface and knead with hands until smooth and elastic. Form a ball, oil and place the dough in a bowl.

- Let it sit, covered, in a warm place to rise. When doubled in size, divide into 6 parts and shape them into balls. Roll each of them into a 20 cm circle.

- Place the naan on a greased baking dish, sprinkle with black seeds and bake in the oven or grill until browned on both sides.

Baked Goods

Crispy Salted Biscuits, AKA Cookies, with Black Seeds

If you're a reader from the UK, understand that we call your biscuits "cookies". To us, a biscuit is a flaky, buttery pastry that we may eat with gravy. Who's more insane? I have no idea. But I do know this recipe involves a combination of sweet and savory, which is pretty crazy by itself.

Servings: 8

DIRECTIONS

- 1 cup all purpose flour
- 120 g butter, softened,
- 3 tbsp confectioner's sugar
- 1 tsp salt
- 1 egg, at room temperature
- 1/4 tsp baking powder
- 1 tsp cardamom powder
- 1 tsp black seeds

DIRECTIONS

- In a bowl, whip the butter and sugar and smooth and creamy. Add the egg and beat well.

- In a separate bowl, combine flour, baking powder, salt and cardamom powder.

- Mix in the egg mixture. Knead to form dough. If the dough is sticky add little flour until it is elastic. Shape the dough onto a ball, slightly oil and wrap with plastic. Refrigerate for an hour.

- When ready to bake, roll out the dough with a rolling pin and cut into circles with a cookie cutter. Sprinkle with black seeds and arrange on a baking sheet lined with parchment.

- Bake at 180 °C for 15 minutes until golden brown.

Baked Goods

Sweet Potato Cookies, I Mean Biscuits

This is the best way we use up leftover sweet potatoes at my house. Often I'll bake sweet potato fries and have them leftover.

Makes 16 biscuits

INGREDIENTS

- 1/4 cup maple syrup
- 1 1/3 cups all purpose flour
- 1 tablespoon baking powder
- 3/4 teaspoon salt
- 1/2 cup unsalted butter, cut into cubes
- 1 large (about 500 g) red-skinned sweet potato (pierced with fork)
- 2/3 cup yellow cornmeal
- 1/2 cup buttermilk
- 1/2 cup pecans (toasted, chopped)
- 1/2 tablespoon black seeds, toasted

DIRECTIONS

- Preheat oven to 230°C

- Cook or microwave the potato until soft. Cut in half and crumble with a fork. Let it cool.

- In a blender, combine the yellow cornmeal, flour, salt and baking powder, add the butter and pulse for a few seconds. Then add the buttermilk, potato, syrup and nuts and blend until smooth.

- Transfer the mixture to a work surface dusted with flour and shape it into a ball. Pat the dough into a circle and cut into 15-16 cookies.

- Arrange them on a baking dish lined with parchment, sprinkle with black seeds and bake in the oven about 20-25 minutes, until light golden and toothpick inserted into center comes out clean.

Gluten Free Cookies with Toasted Black seeds

I don't think I can appease my UK audience anymore—they're cookies, dammit!

Servings: 5

INGREDIENTS

- 2 eggs
- 1/4 cup vegetable oil
- 1/4 cup sugar
- 1 1/4 cups gluten-free flour
- 3 tablespoons baking powder
- 1 cup cornmeal
- 1 cup milk
- 1/2 teaspoon salt
- 1 teaspoon black seeds

DIRECTIONS

- Preheat the oven to 225 °C. Combine the cornmeal, flour, baking powder, sugar and salt in a medium mixing bowl.

- Whisk in the oil, eggs and milk. Mix well to form soft dough.

- Lightly coat a work surface with flour. Transfer the dough on it and roll out into a thin round (about 2 cm thickness).

- Cut the dough into 10 cookies using a cookie cutter. Arrange them on a lightly greased baking sheet, sprinkle with black seeds and bake in the oven for 10- 12 minutes until golden brown and firm to the touch.

Cheesy Cornbread

By now you're an expert at cooking with black seeds. They taste good in almost any savory baked good, just as you'd expect from sesame or poppy seeds. Cornbread tastes especially good with them.

Servings: 8

INGREDIENTS

- 2 cups buttermilk
- 1 large egg
- 3 tsp vegetable oil
- 1 3/4 cups self-rising yellow cornmeal
- 2 cups sharp shredded Cheddar cheese
- 1 tsp nigella seeds

DIRECTIONS

- Preheat oven to 230° C. Grease a round or square rimmed baking dish with vegetable oil and place in the oven for 5 minutes until heated well.

- Toast some nigella seeds, through the standard nigella seed toasting process.

- Meanwhile in a medium bowl, combine the egg, cornmeal, buttermilk and cheese. Then the seeds. Stir well and pour the mixture into the rimmed pan.

- Bake the corn bread 25 minutes. Let stand in the pan for 5 minutes, then cut slice and serve.

Black Seed Flavored Flatbreads

Fresh and tasty flatbreads flavored with toasted black seeds. They are super-easy to make.

Servings: 8

INGREDIENTS

- 1 ¼ cup natural yogurt
- Pinch of salt
- 400g all purpose flour, plus extra for dusting
- 1 tbsp black seeds, toasted

DIRECTIONS

- Heat the grill to medium. Coat a baking dish with flour. In a medium bowl combine the black seeds and flour, season with a pinch of salt. Then add the yogurt and 1/3 cup wate.

- Mix well to form soft dough.

- Divide into 8 parts. Roll out each of the balls into ovals or circles and arrange on the prepared baking sheet.

- Lightly sprinkle with flour and grill for about 4-5 minutes per side until light brown and puffed. Enjoy warm.

Black Seed Cupcakes

It takes only 25 minutes to make these adorable cupcakes. Enjoy them with a cup of tea or coffee.

Servings: 12

INGREDIENTS

- 1 cup all-purpose flour
- 1 teaspoon baking powder
- 1/2 teaspoon salt
- 1/4 teaspoon baking soda
- 2 tbsp butter
- 1 tbsp extra-light olive oil
- 1/2 cup granulated sugar
- 1 large egg
- 1 large egg white
- 2 tsp lemon rind, grated
- 1/2 cup buttermilk
- 2 tbsp black seeds

DIRECTIONS

- Preheat oven to 175 °C. Coat 12 muffin cups with cooking spray, or line with parchment papers.

- Combine the butter and oil in a bowl and mix well, gradually adding the granulated sugar. Beat well. Add one egg, followed by the egg white.

- Next, mix in the lemon rind. In a separate bowl, combine the flour, baking powder, soda and salt and add to the egg mixture.

- Finally mix in the black seeds.

Baked Goods

- Pour the mixture into muffin cups and bake in the oven for 20-22 minutes, until t a toothpick inserted in the center comes out clean. Transfer the pan to a wire rack to cool.

- Enjoy.

Cheddar Scones

We finish this book with some scones. Cheddar cheese and black seeds work together in this quasi-healthy recipe to provide a yummy flavor. I'll see you later!

Servings: 12-14

INGREDIENTS

400 g all purpose flour
4 tbsp low fat natural yogurt
4 tsp xanthan gum
150 g butter
2 tsp baking powder
2 tsp dijon mustard
Pinch salt
80 g potato starch
2 large eggs, beate
2 tsp black seeds
3 ½ oz. (100 g) cheddar, grated
½ cup (100ml) milk

DIRECTIONS

- Preheat oven to 220 ° C. Line a baking sheet with parchment.

- In a bowl combine the flour, cornstarch, baking powder, butter, xanthan gum. Season the mixture with a pinch of salt and mix well. Then stir in the grated cheddar and black seeds.

- Combine the beaten eggs, yogurt, milk and mustard in another bowl then add to the flour mixture. Now knead the dough with your hands to form soft dough. Add some more milk if the dough is a bit dry.

- Coat a work surface with flour, transfer the dough onto it and knead until smooth. Roll it out into a thin circle. Cut out the scones with a cutter and arrange on a baking sheet.

- Brush the tops with milk or egg (if desired), season with cayenne pepper, and bake in the oven for about 15 minutes until golden brown. Transfer the scones to a wire rack and let them cool.

A Message from Andrea

Thank you so much for taking the time to read this book. I hope that this was of some benefit to you.

You can find many more books like this one I've created by checking out my Amazon page at the following address:
http://www.amazon.com/Andrea-Silver/e/B00W820AR6/.

You can also get in touch with me personally at AndreaSilverWellness@gmail.com if you have any questions or ideas.

Manufactured by Amazon.ca
Bolton, ON

29457433R00055